For Mike
fellow teacher
(team teacher)
Fondly,
Aram
4/28/07

ARAM SAROYAN

COMPLETE MINIMAL POEMS

UGLY DUCKLING PRESSE
LOST LITERATURE SERIES
NEW YORK

©2007 UDP

Published by Ugly Duckling Presse
www.uglyducklingpresse.org

ISBN - 13: 978-1-933254-25-8

Edited by Aram Saroyan and James Hoff
Designed by William Bahan

Text set in Adobe Casion

Printed in Michigan by McNaughton & Gunn, Inc.

This publication was partially funded by a grant
from the National Endowment for the Arts.

NATIONAL
ENDOWMENT
FOR THE ARTS

Library of Congress CIP data is available upon request

Table of Contents

ARAM SAROYAN

a man stands
on his
head one
minute--

then he
sit
down all
different

whistling in the street a car turning in the room ticking

a leaf
left
by the
cat
I guess

the noises of the garden among the noises of the room

a window to walk away
in

$$\begin{array}{r} \text{ocean} \\ + \ \underline{\text{forest}} \\ \text{horses} \end{array}$$

night
again
again

my knees are in my knees
my eyes are in my eyes

sky
every
day

ex-
track
coach
dies

Pablo
Picasso
and
Casals.

a dish
of Irish
setters

wind   o i l   to
blows   out   sea

Happy
Birthday

Happy
Wedding

Anniversary

My arms are warm

Aram Saroyan

STEAK

ABCDEFGHIJKLMNOPQRSTUVWXYZ

W A B C
W A D O
W B A I
W B N X
W C B S
W D H A
W E V D
W F A S
W F M E
W F Y I
W F U V
W H B I
W H L I
WHOM
W H N
W I N S
W J R Z
W K C R
W L I B
W L I R
WMCA
W N B C
W N C N
WNEW
W N J R
W N Y C
W N Y E
W O R
W P A T
W P I X
WPOW
W Q X R
W R F M
W R V R
W S O U
WTFM
W V I P
W V N J
W V O X
WWRL

m

crickets
crickets
crickets
crickets
crickets
crickets
crickets
crickets
crickets
crickets
crickets
crickets
crickets
crickets
crickets
crickets
crickets
crickets
crickcts
crickets
crickets
crickets
crickets
crickets
crickets
crickets
crickets
crickets
crickets
crickets
crickets
crickets
crickets
crickets
crickets
crickets
crickets
crickets
crickets
crickets
crickets
crickets
crickets
crickets
crickets

eyeye

lighght

morni,ng

Blod

coffee
coffee

bird
bird
bird

silence
silence

,
aren't

fall over

fall over

fall over

fall over

ly   ly

ly   ly

o   r

o   r

PAGES

POEMS
1964-1965
New York

POEM

One two
three there
are three are
never seen
again.

OLD POEM

I make another room
smaller
in this one

          --there--

is all I want.
Carry over to it

   the ashtray

POEM

A new
telephone
on the table.

"If I really see anything,
I hear it too."

A new telephone on the table.

TWO SENTENCES

1. I'm trying to write a poem.

2. The broom is in the corner.

FEBRUARY'S GONE

on this machine.

TRAVEL

I went all across country
A sense of humor
The size of farm animals.

A POEM TO K.Q.

I'm going to kill you.

Had West followed up her fine opening lead by dropping the club king or queen on the second round of clubs, she would have been able to play the ten when Stayman tried to throw her in. Then East could have overtaken and returned a heart, wrecking the contract.

MOVING

The floor passing through the hole in the bag
I smell of you!

5 POEMS
1964-1965
New York

BUS RIDE

1

a red tractor
a red tractor
etcetera

2

fences   /   finished

TWO POEMS

A PENNY	1¢
A PENNY	1¢
A PENNY	1¢
A PENNY	1¢
A PENNY	+ 1¢
A NICKEL	5¢

A NICKEL	5¢
A NICKEL	+ 5¢
A DIME	10¢

A DIME	10¢
A DIME	10¢
A NICKEL	+ 5¢
A QUARTER	25¢

A QUARTER	25¢
A QUARTER	+ 25¢
FIFTY CENTS	50¢

FIFTY CENTS	50¢
FIFTY CENTS	+ 50¢
ONE DOLLAR	100¢ = $1

w w w w

w w w w

· · · ·

w a w w

w a k w

w a k e

· · · ·

w a l w

w a l k

Poem Recognizing Someone In The Street

e y ? h
e ? h e
h e y !

crickets
crickess
cricksss
cricssss
crisssss
crsssss
cssssss
ssssssss
sssssts
sssssets
sssskets
sssckets
ssickets
srickets
crickets

SLED HILL VOICES
Summer 1965
Woodstock, New York

Not a
cricket

ticks a
clock

something moving in the garden a cat

Sunday

as the
grass's
cut

and its smell
rises
twice

incomprehensible birds

what energy pops
            flops her
    on her back
            laughing
        in the water

the noises of the garden among the noises of the room

THIRD FLOOR VOICES
Fall 1965
New York

a voice only
audible
below

closer
someone speaks
Spanish

the radiator, the radio louder

a car roars over a
conversation

whistling in the street a car turning in the room ticking

5 POEMS
1966-1967
New York
Cambridge, Mass.

Insist
on
certain
things.

Car Swerves,
Injures 11;
Driver Held

room now
door Humphrey
Bogart

cat
book
city

Ted Ted Ted Ted
Ted

POEMS
1966-1967
New York
London
Stockholm
Cambridge, Mass.

sing, swim, sing

priit

I crazy.

.   .   .

ian hamilton finlay

aaple

lobstee

torgh

Alice

ney
mo
money

night
so daylight

SHORT POEMS

Placitas

to L. Z.

The trees'
noise of
the sea.

N.Y.C.

I keep seeing Italy down the street.

Marijuana Notation

my eyes--
back there
in the mirror
where I left them

A B C

Louder in the dark.

JULY

It'll hit you you in July.

Later

the atelier

ate her.

In the corner of my room an American!

stones
from off
the top
of rocks

take them down and throw them away

left
face

right
face

about
face

everybody
loves
a poet

a poet
loves
everybody

I see
this
little

and
even
less.

Sausalito, California
is the home
of a friend of mine,
Mr. Richard Kolmar

My cup is yellow
Or not, though not's

Impossible
It's yellow

The scissors was on the newspaper where who would ever see it.

It may
be the
coffee-
maker

or it
may be
the ra-
diator.

LONDON

I sleep around the
pillow in the light
yellow morning, a member
of the avant-garde.

SONG

My father's my father's,
my mother's my mother's,
my sister's my sister's,
I'm, I'm, I'm, I'm, I'm.

QUOTE

Oh, peaceful room,
peaceful blanket,
large pillow, cold,
interesting art...

PLACID TEAS

The cream
made an "e"
in the tea.

GAILYN

sits
at the
window

LOUIS

Noisy
"Zukofsky"

COUPON

Coupons are the brightest yellowest
Reddest headiest delights on the face of the earth!

PLAY

Father: Speak English Today.
Son: Allright.

LYRIC

I'm a cardboard poet.
I eat rice.

American coins
are more interesting
in England.

How strange
money is on
L.S.D.

Be sure
before you
forget.

We made a raincoat
for a bee.

My orchestra
is
ready.

a joint
open
hearing

opera
of the nervous
system

an oyster
can't
read this

traffic
an airplane
the typewriter

a cartoon
of
energy

pool
of
fluff

aunt;
&
uncle.

a d j
u s t
men
t . .

suc
cess

1, 2, 3, 4, 5, 6, 7, 8, 9, 10, 11, 12, 13, 14, 15, 16, 17, 18, 19, 20.

one
two
three

t

n

y

y
ou

tinker-toy-dream

oh oh oh oh oh oh oh oh oh

suggest bear

oh oh oh oh oh oh oh oh oh

LOVELY

l o v e l y

BOXING MATCH

. . . .
. . . .
. . . .
. . . .
. . . .
. . . .
. . . .
. . . .

POEM

PL 5-4782

YU 8-4973

GR 4-6527

EL 5-9573

GR 5-4374

THE COLLECTED WORKS

```
"  #  $  %  _  &  '  (   )  *  !
2  3  4  5  6  7  8  9  0  -  ¾

Q  W  E  R  T  Y  U  I  O  P  ¼
q  w  e  r  t  y  u  i  o  p  ½

A  S  D  F  G  H  J  K  L  :  @
a  s  d  f  g  h  j  k  l  ;  ¢

Z  X  C  V  B  N  M  ,  .  ?
z  x  c  v  b  n  m  ,  .  /
```

ELECTRIC POEMS

j;u;n;g;l;e

pagne
cham.

eatc.

even
even
even
even
even
even
seven

nnausea

z/o/x

Judd…

Big thoughts.

Shakespeare!

YOU YOU

PAUL KLee

ht night night night night night night night night night night night night nig

ight night night night night night night night night night night night night night ni

tick

tick

22
22
22
22
22
22
22
22
22
22
22
22
22
22
22
22
22
22
22
22
22
22
22
22
22
22
22
22
22
22
22
22
22
22
22
22
22
22
22
22
22
22

23
23
23
23
23
23
23
23
23
23
23
23
23
23
23
23
23
23
23
23
23
23
23
23
23
23
23
23
23
23
23
23
23
23
23
23
23
23
23
23
23
23

i i i i i i i i i i i i i i i i i i i i i i i i i i i i i i i i i i i i i i i i i i i i i i i i i i i i i i i i i i i i i i i i i i

i i i i i i i i i i i i i i i i i i i i i i i i i i i i i i i i i i i i i i i i i i i i i i i i i i i i i i i i i i i i i i i i i i i i

THE REST

SLED HILL VOICES
Summer 1965
Woodstock, New York

JULY POEM

a single hissing bird
   trees hissing
     --it's raining--?

     .

this morning birds a million's
    noises one in
      another's
          "an infinity"

    .

HONKS
               hissing

water for tea

Tied to a tree
     together
one Barking

The other has a bad ear
Squeals
at him

Outside
a jet I can't see--

a dog.

a lawn mower ? in my ear

near &
far birds

a fly very
Close

I leaps

through
my eyes

the trees

destroyed
in water

THIRD FLOOR VOICES
Fall 1965
New York City

After rain

a woman walks
below cars and a

truck (rattles)
tread through

the water
left over

the clock clicking
heels

in the street
something

knocks
in the wall

somebody as

suddenly as a radio comes on
in the street

speaks

In all the white the wall is

is so tiny a
black crawling roach--a

distance in and out of
vision.

SONGS & BUTTONS
1966
New York/London

Life is
sweet--

it's
delicious.

L.B.J.
is
Ugly.

Money
doesn't grow
on trees.

Banana?
No.
Orange?
No.
Peach?
No.
Apple?
Yes.

Ron Padgett
would approve
this idea.

trees
roots
grass

corporate pirates

leukemia

guarantee

Paul Klee
is dead.

hghgh

noom

waht

black salad

toy sores

HAPPY!!!
INSTANT!

REMIEIMBER

FAICE

Doctor Ornette

e
like

Picassc

oxygen

gum

ARAM SAROYAN
Fall--Winter 1966
Cambridge, Mass.

eights

dimes animal

wire air

secretary trees

pencil coin

typewriter kittens

when plum

every days

six
very

table
ambulance

ink
suit
ice

air
rice
fur

farm
eye
month

sea
noun
clips

ask
born
cigarette

lit
envelope
hungry

arm
wheat
mile
egg

CAMBRIDGE PIECES
1967
Cambridge, Mass.

seek

air

tragedy

bodies

OF

hammer & mile

all   all

all   all

children children

chariot

chariot

cowboy

cowboy

polite

polite

oxygen

oxygen

THE REST
Summer 1970
Marblehead, Mass.

one

two

three

four

five

arx

seven

light

nine

ten

a bird flies by.

children scream.

Gailyn is doing the dishes.

ACKNOWLEDGMENTS

Much of the work in Complete Minimal Poems first appeared, in sequences duplicated here, in the following books: Aram Saroyan (Random House, 1968), Pages (Random House, 1969), and The Rest (Telegraph, 1971). "Electric Poems" was printed in the anthology All Stars (Goliard/Grossman, New York, 1972), edited by Tom Clark. The section "Short Poems" appears here for the first time in book form.

Before their appearance in the larger collections above, many of these poems were printed in the following chapbooks: Poems (with Jenni Caldwell and Richard Kolmar), Acadia Press, New York, 1964; In, A Bear Press Book, Eugene, OR, 1965; Works, Lines Press, New York, 1965; Sled Hill Voices, Goliard Press, U.K., 1966; Aram Saroyan, Lines Press, Cambridge, MA, 1967; and By Air Mail (with Victor Bockris), Strange Faeces Press, London, 1972.

Many of the poems also appeared, originally or subsequently, in the following publications: 0 to 9, 0 To 9: The Complete Magazine 1967-1969 (Ugly Duckling Presse, Brooklyn, 2006), 34th Street, Adventures in Poetry, The Agents of Impurity (Sonic Arts Network, UK, 2004), The American Literary Anthology 1 (Farrar Straus & Giroux, New York, 1968), The American Literary Anthology 2 (Random House, New York, 1969), Anthology of Concrete Poetry (Something Else Press, New York, 1967), Anthology of Concretism (The Swallow Press, Chicago, 1969), An Anthology of New York Poets (Random House, New York, 1970), Angel Hair, Another World (Bobbs-Merrill, 1971), A Poke in the I: A Collection of Concrete Poems (Candlewick Press, Cambridge, Mass., 2001), Art and Literature, before your very eyes! (U.K.), Art News Annual (Macmillan, New York, 1969), The Boston Phoenix, C, The Chicago Review, Concrete Poetry: A World View (University of Indiana Press, Bloomington, 1969), Concrete Poetry in Europe, Canada, and America (Editions Hansjorg Mayer, Stuttgart, 1966), The Discovery of Poetry (Harcourt, 2001), Drainage, Elephant, Era, Grande Ronde Review, Gum, Hellcoal Annual One, Hispanic Arts, ICA Bulletin (U.K.), Joglars, Les Lettres (France), Les Levine's Poem Disposables (Museum of Modern Art, New York, 1969), Lines, Mother (Pittsburgh), Nadada, or/oar, OnceAgain (New Directions, New York, 1968), The Paris Review, The Paris Review Anthology (Norton, New York, 1990), Patterns, Poets at Le Metro, Poor. Old. Tired. Horse. (Scotland), Rolling Stone, Search for Tomorrow, Shake the Kaleidoscope (Pocket Books, New York, 1973), Telegrams, This, This Book Is a Movie (Delta Books, New York, 1971), Tom Clark's Once Series, The World, and The Young American Poets (Big Table-Follett, Chicago, 1968).

Poems in this collection have appeared in the following textbooks: An Introduction to Poetry (Little Brown, 1978), The Discovery of Poetry: A Field Guide to Reading and Writing Poems (College Edition, Harcourt, 1987)), How Porcupines Make Love (Xerox, 1972), Patterns of Language (American Book Company, 1974), The Poem as Process (Harcourt Brace Jovanovich, 1974), Poems (Houghton Mifflin, 1973), Probes: An Introduction to Poetry (Macmillan, 1973), and Since Feeling Is First (Scott Foresman, 1971),

The following poems first appeared in Poetry: A Magazine of Verse: in the September 1966 issue: "Not a/cricket"; "the noises of the garden..."; "the

trees//destroyed"; "Sunday"; in the September 1967 issue: "sky…", "a dish…", "I crazy", "room now…","cham./pagne"; "j;u;n;g;l;e", "Car Swerves";" seek/ air…";"wind/blows…"; and in the June 1968 issue: "night night night…"

There are recorded versions of two poems, "crickets/crickets/crickets…" and "WBAI/ WBNX…", on Mother 9: The Album Issue (New York, 1968); "Not a/cricket" on The Dial-a-Poem Poets (Giorno Poetry Systems, 1973): and "crickets/crickets/ crickets…" on 10+2: 12 American Text Sound Pieces (1750 Arch Records, Berkeley, 1975; resissued as a CD by Other Minds, San Francisco, 2003), and Loud 5 (2007)

Grateful acknowledgment is made to
the publishers and editors responsible.

Ugly Duckling Presse would like to thank
Danny Snelson for his work and contributions
to this publication.